MANUSCRIPT PAPER.

MANUSCRIPT PAPER.

Amsco Publications
London / New York / Sydney

Order No. AM 40486
International Standard Book Number: 0.8256.2117.8

Printed in the United States of America

Notation

Musical tones are represented on a written or printed page by characters called *Notes*.
They appear on a group of five horizontal lines called a *Staff*.
The type of note explains its *Time Value*.
The position of the note on the staff denotes its *Pitch*.
Notes too high or too low to be placed on the staff appear on short added lines below or above it called *Ledger* lines.
Below is shown the staff with its ledger lines:

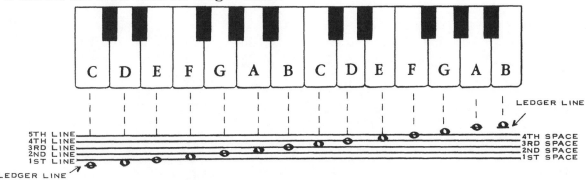

Types of notes with comparative time values are:

Whole Note (o) = 2 Half Notes (d)	Half Note (d) = 2 Quarter Notes (♩)
Quarter Note (♩) = 2 8th Notes (♪)	8th Note (♪) = 2 16th Notes (♬)
16th Note (♬) = 2 32nd Notes (♬)	32nd Note (♬) = 2 64th Notes (♬)

Eighth notes and notes of shorter duration in time can be joined together in groups by cross bars called *Beams*.

```
1 beam    2 beams   3 beams   4 beams
```

Specific pitch of notes is indicated by letter-names using the first 7 letters of the alphabet.

A *Clef* sign appearing at the beginning of the staff fixes the pitch or letter-name of one particular note and letter-names to follow.

Treble Clef (G Clef) fixes G on the 2nd line

Bass Clef (F Clef) fixes F on the 4th line

These are the clefs most commonly used.
The piano and other keyboard instruments use the *Treble* (right hand) and the *Bass Clef* (left hand) at the same time.

The example below shows many of the notes with their letter-names in Bass and Treble clefs.

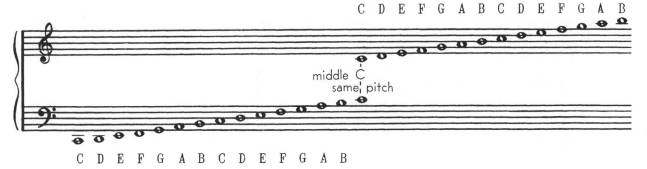

Rests (periods of silence) have time values equal to notes of the same name.

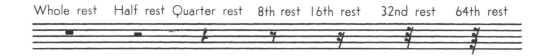

| Whole rest | Half rest | Quarter rest | 8th rest | 16th rest | 32nd rest | 64th rest |

Whole Rest (▬) = 2 Half Rests (▬)   Half Rest   (▬) = 2 Quarter Rests (𝄽)
Quarter Rest (𝄽) = 2 8th Rests   (𝄾)   8th Rest   (𝄾) = 2 16th Rests   (𝄿)
16th Rest   (𝄿) = 2 32nd Rests (𝅀)   32nd Rest (𝅀) = 2 64th Rests   (𝅁)

A *Dot* after a note or rest increases its time value by one-half.
For example, a dotted half note (𝅗𝅥.) = in time value 3 quarter notes.

Music is divided by vertical lines called *Bars* (or bar lines) into portions called *Measures*.

The total time value in each measure is shown at the beginning of the music by a time signature consisting of an upper and lower number. The upper indicates the number of counts (beats) within each measure; the lower number explains the time value of each count.

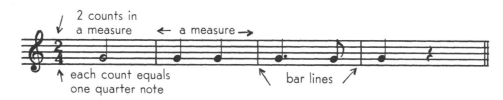

Common time signatures: $\dfrac{2}{4}$ $\dfrac{3}{4}$ $\dfrac{4}{4}$ $\dfrac{3}{8}$ $\dfrac{6}{8}$ $\dfrac{9}{8}$ $\dfrac{12}{8}$

Special time signatures: $C = \dfrac{4}{4}$ $\mathrm{\mathbb{C}} = \dfrac{2}{2}$ (cut time, called *alla breve.*)

One complete measure of rest, regardless of time signature, is indicated by a whole rest (▬).

Several measures of rest are indicated by a number.

This means 22 measures of rest.

A double bar shows the end of a composition or portion of it.

repeat the music in between

A section of the music to be played twice is indicated as follows:

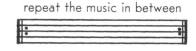

Sometimes a repeated passage has a different closing when played the second time.
In this instance first and second endings are used:

First ending   Second ending

%. means repeat the previous measure.

——————————— indicates a gradual increase in volume (loudness) called *crescendo.*

——————————— shows a gradual decrease in volume called *decrescendo* or *diminuendo.*

A dot over or under a note (♩ ♪)—*staccato*—means to cut it short leaving a gap of silence between it and the next note if there be one.

A curved line ⌒ called a *Slur* means to play the contained notes in a smooth and connected manner called *Legato.*

If a similar curved line appears between notes of the same pitch it is called a *Tie* and adds the time value of the tied notes together producing in effect one longer note.

Sharps and *Flats* are placed before notes to raise or lower their pitch.

♯ —raises the note one half-step
♭ —lowers the note one half-step
♮ —cancels the sharp or flat; restores note to original pitch
𝄪 —raises the note two half-steps
♭♭—lowers the note two half-steps

The chromatic signs shown above when appearing within the body of the music are called *Accidentals.* Once one appears, an accidental has the same effect on all notes of the same letter-name appearing in the same measure unless contradicted by a different accidental. If not specifically cancelled the effect of an accidental on a tied note is carried into the next measure.

When all notes of a certain letter-name are to be played sharp or flat, the information is given as a key signature appearing at the beginning of the music—directly to the right of the clef sign. Each key signature can indicate a major key having a major scale, or a minor key (with a different name) having a minor scale. The key-note (main note) of the minor scale is always three half-steps lower than the key-note of the major scale with the same key signature.

Below are shown a few common key signatures and scales.

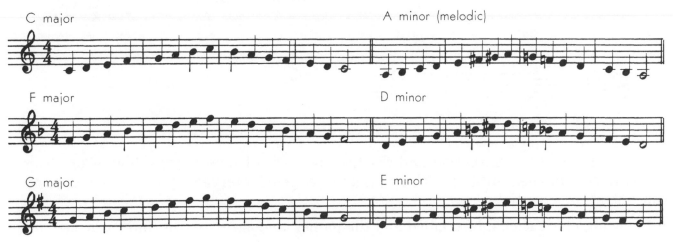

C major   A minor (melodic)

F major   D minor

G major   E minor

Other key signatures are shown below:

Changes of key frequently occur within a musical composition.

To change from a sharp or flat key to the key of C draw double bar lines and show naturals specifically cancelling the sharps or flats in the old key.

To change to a new key with additional sharps or flats draw a double bar line and indicate the new key signature.

To change to a new key with fewer sharps or flats draw double bar lines and write in naturals specifically cancelling the sharps or flats to be dropped; then show the sharps or flats to be retained.

To change from a sharp to a flat key (or the reverse) write in naturals after the double bar lines cancelling the entire old signature; then write in new signature.

If the music in the first key reaches to the end of a line (which is preferable), show the key change after the double bar lines at the end of the line, leaving the end open and write in at the beginning of the next line only the new key signature.

Examples:

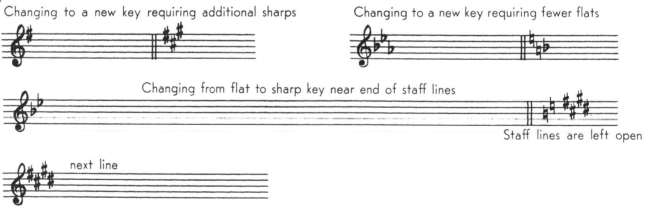

To understand chord construction and the transposition of music into a higher or lower key for instruments pitched in Bb, Eb, F, etc., a knowledge of intervals (the vertical distance between notes) is essential.

The following chart should be studied and the names and sizes of the intervals memorized.

Abbreviations used in naming the intervals:
M — Major   m — minor   Aug. — augmented   Dim. — diminished   P — perfect

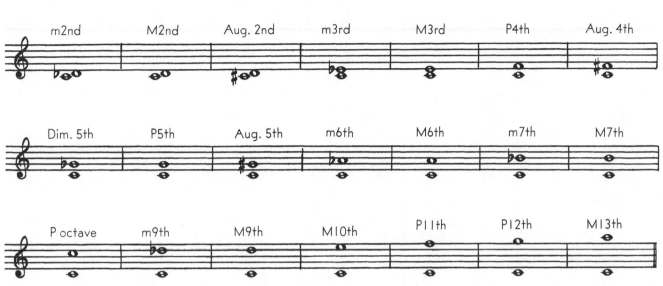

Chords are groups of three or more notes played at the same time. They are named according to the intervals between the notes used. On the next page is a reference chart showing the chords in most common use.

Each chord has a name consisting of the letter-name of the root (the note upon which the chord is built) plus a symbol showing its kind or type. If no symbol is shown—only the root letter—the chord is major. Other symbols are:

m — minor   + — augmented   6 — major sixth   m6 — minor sixth   7 — dominant seventh

m7 — minor seventh   ma7 — major seventh   o — diminished seventh   9 — dominant ninth

The rate of speed or *Tempo* is indicated at the beginning of a musical composition. The most commonly used tempo markings are:

adagio *(ah DAH jo)*—slow
agitato *(ah je TAH to)*—agitated
allegretto *(ah leh GRET to)*—rather lively
allegro *(ah LEH gro)*—lively fast
andante *(ahn DAHN teh)*—rather slow
andantino *(ahn dahn TEE no)*—a little faster than andante
a tempo *(ah TEM po)*—at the original speed
comodo *(CO mo do)*—easy, convenient
con brio *(cohn BREE o)*—with dash

dim.-diminuendo *(dim in oo EN do)*—gradually getting softer
moderato *(mo deh RAH to)*—at a moderate speed
nicht schnell *(nisht SHNEL)*—not fast
scherzo *(SKEHRT so)*—a joke or humorous composition
teneramente *(ten ehr ah MEN teh)*—tenderly
tranquillo *(tran QUEEL lo)*—tranquilly, quietly
vivace *(vee VAH cheh)*—very lively, fast
vivo *(VEE vo)*—lively

A more definite method to indicate the tempo is by means of a metronome marking. Show the type of note to be considered as one count or beat, then the number at which the metronome should be set to get the desired tempo. For example: ♩ =112.

Reference Chart Of Common Chords

Instrument Ranges

To write a part for any musical instrument it is necessary to know its range. If the instrument is pitched in a key other than C, the correct transposition must be made. The range and transposition for some of the more common instruments are shown below.

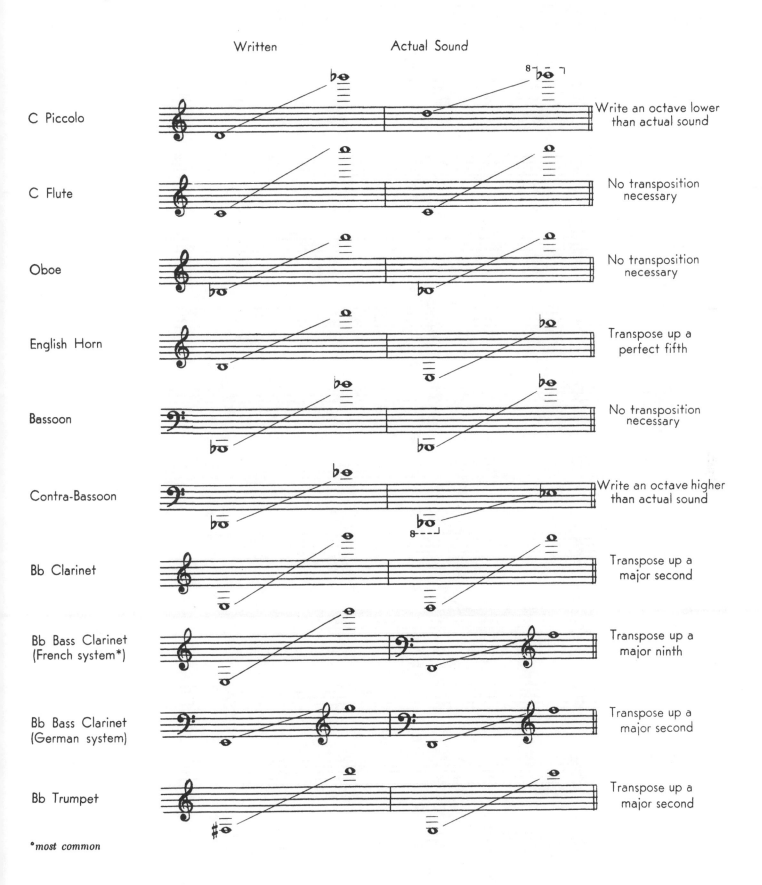

*most common

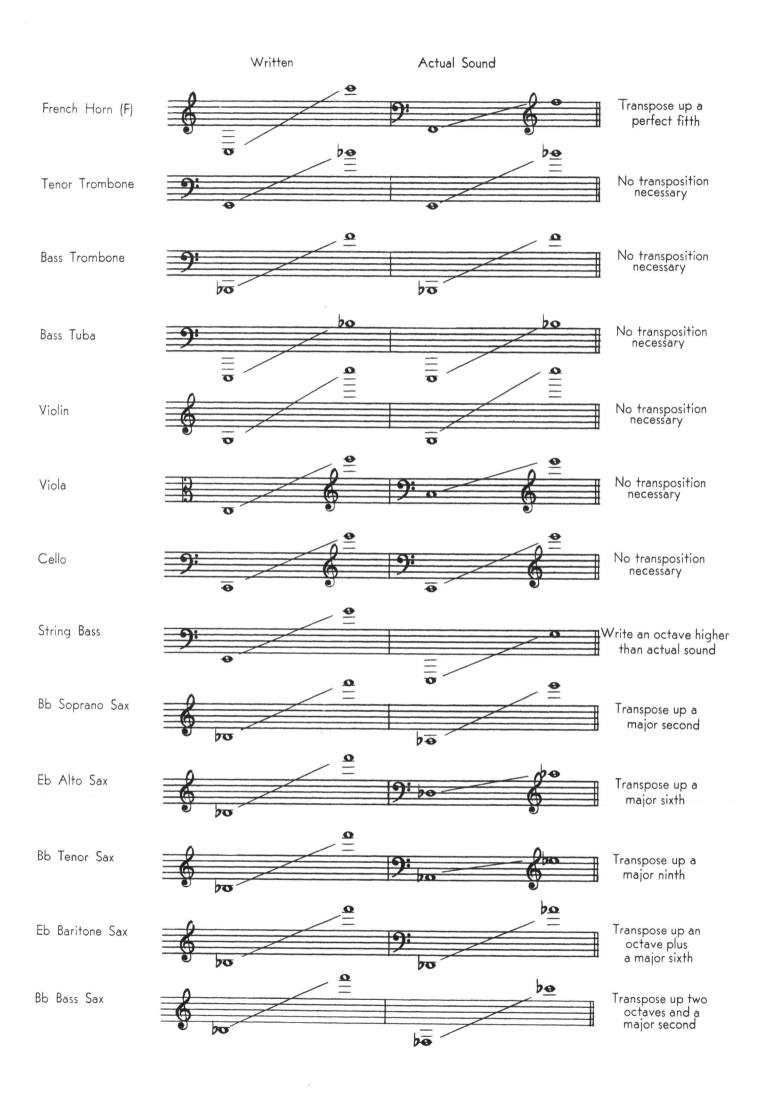

Dictionary Of Musical Terms

A—to, at, in
accelerando (*accel.*)—growing faster
accent—emphasis placed on a note or chord
adagio—slowly
a deux (*a 2*)—to be played by both instruments
ad libitum (*ad lib.*)—freely; not in strict time
affettuoso—with feeling and emotion
agitato—agitated, restless, hurried
al fine—to the end
alla—in the style of
alla breve (¢)—cut time; two beats to the measure; one beat to each half note
allargando (*allarg.*)—growing slower and louder
allegretto—a bright tempo; faster than moderato but slower than allegro
allegro—fast
amoroso—affectionately
andante—a moderately slow but flowing tempo
andantino—a little faster than andante
animato—animated; with spirit
a piacere—at pleasure; equivalent of *ad libitum*
appassionato—with passion and emotion
appoggiatura—a grace note which takes the accent and part of the time value of the following principal note; often called long grace note
arpeggio—notes of a chord played consecutively; a broken chord
assai—very
a tempo—in the original tempo
attacca—begin the next portion of the music without pausing
bassa—low. 8va bassa means play the notes an octave lower than written
ben—well
bis—twice; repeat the passage
bravura—boldness
brillante—brilliant
brio—vigor, spirit
cadenza—an elaborate solo passage, frequently unaccompanied, used as an embellishment
calando—gradually softer and slower
cantabile—in a singing style
capriccioso—in a fanciful and capricious style
chromatic—proceeding by semitones (half steps)
coda—a closing passage
con, col—with
con anima—with animation and boldness
con brio—with vigor and brilliancy
con espressione—with expression
con fuoco—with fire and passion
con moto—with motion
con spirito—with spirit and energy
crescendo (*cresc.*)—increasing the volume or loudness of the tone
da, dal—from
da capo (*D.C.*)—from the beginning

D.C. al fine—from the beginning to the word *Fine* (*the finish or end*)
dal segno (*D.S.*)—from the sign ⊕
D.S. al fine—from the sign to the word *Fine*
decrescendo (*decresc.*)—decreasing the volume of the tone
diminuendo (*dim.*)—gradually softer
divisi (*div.*)—divided; each part to be played by a separate instrument
dolce—sweetly
dolcissimo—very sweetly
dolore—sorrow, sadness
doloroso—sadly
dynamics—expression produced by the different degrees of volume of the tone
E—and
elegante—elegant, graceful
energico—energetic, vigorous
enharmonic—alike in pitch but different in notation
espressivo—expressively
fermata (⌢)—a pause or hold
finale—the concluding movement
fine—the end
forte (*f*)—loud
forte-piano (*fp*)—accent strongly, diminishing immediately to piano
fortissimo (*ff*)—very loud
forza—force, power, strength
forzando (*fz*)—the note or chord strongly accented
fuoco—fire, energy
furioso—furious
giocoso—humorous
giojoso—joyous
giusto—exact; in strict time
glissando—slurred smoothly in a gliding manner
grace notes—small notes added for an ornamental or embellishing effect
grandioso—in a grand manner
grave—solemnly and very slowly
grazioso—gracefully
gruppetto—a group of grace notes; a turn
il—the
impetuoso—impetuous
key note—the tonic or first note in a scale
lamentoso—lamenting, sad
largamente—in a full, broad style
larghetto—slowly, but not as slowly as largo
largo—a slow, broad tempo
ledger lines—short lines added above or below the staff for notes too high or too low to appear on or within the staff
legato—in a smooth, connected manner, indicated by the slur
leggiero—lightly
lento—slow

l'istesso tempo—at the same tempo as the previous passage or movement

loco—as written; generally used after a passage marked 8 va

ma—but

ma non troppo—but not too much so

maestoso—majestic, dignified

maggiore—the major key

marcato—in a marked and emphatic style

marcia—march

marziale—in a martial style

meno—less

meno mosso—less motion; slower

mezzo—half

mezzo forte (*mf*)—moderately loud

mezzo piano (*mp*)—moderately soft

minore—the minor key

misterioso—mysteriously

moderato—moderately

molto—much, very

mordent—an embellishment of two or more notes that make up a very short trill

morendo—dying away; softer and softer

mosso—movement

moto—motion

non—not

non tanto—not too much

notation—the art of representing music by written or printed characters (notes, rests, etc.)

obbligato—a counter-melody which complements the main theme and which constitutes an indispensable part of the composition

octave—an interval of eight diatonic sounds; notes an octave apart have the same letter name, but one of them is higher than the other

opus—a work or composition

ossia—otherwise; or else: indicating another way of playing a passage

ottava (*8va.*)—to be played an octave higher

passionato—passionate

patetico—pathetic

pause (⌒)—a pause, also called hold or fermata

perdendosi—gradually softer and slower; dying away.

pianissimo (*pp*)—very softly

piano (*p*)—softly

piu—more, as piu forte, piu lento, etc.

piu mosso—more movement; faster

poco—a little.

poco a poco—little by little

pomposo—pompous, grand

prestissimo—as fast as possible

presto—very fast; faster than allegro

primo (*1mo*)—the first, as Tempo Primo

quasi—like; in the style of

rallentando (*rall.*)—gradually slower

recitativo (*recit.*)—a style of performance intended to sound like a dramatic recitation in natural speech.

replica—repetition

rinforzando (*rfz.*)—reinforced; played with added strength and emphasis.

risoluto—in a resolute and bold manner

ritardando (*rit.*)—retarding; gradually slowing the tempo

ritenuto (*riten.*)—in a slower tempo; held back

rubato—robbing or taking from the notes their strict time value by alternately hurrying and retarding for the purpose of expression

scherzando—playfully

segue—follows on; continue

semplice—in a simple, unaffected manner

sempre—always, continually

senza—without

sforzando (*sfz.*)—with sudden force or emphasis

simile—similarly; in like manner

smorzando (*smorz.*)—extinguished; suddenly dying away

solo—a composition or passage for a single voice or instrument

sordino—a mute, such as used for a violin, a trumpet

sostenuto—sustained

sotto voce—in a quiet, subdued tone

spirito—spirit, energy

staccato—detached; cut short

stringendo (*string.*)—pressing; accelerating the tempo

subito—immediately, suddenly

syncopation—a type of time structure in which an accented note occurs on an ordinarily weak beat and is prolonged through an ordinarily strong beat

tacet—be silent; do not play

tempo—rate of speed

tenuto (*ten.*)—held for the full time value

tranquillo—quietly, calmly

tremolo—repetition of a note or chord with great rapidity producing a tremulous sound

trill—a rapid alternation between the printed note and the next note above it

triplet—a group of three notes played in the time usually given to two notes of the same value

troppo—too much

turn (∿)—an embellishment consisting of four rapidly played notes that wind around the printed note

tutti—all together

un—a, one, an

vivace—lively, briskly

vivo—animated, quick

volti subito (*v.s.*)—turn the page immediately

Notes

Notes